JAZZ
Legends

WRITTEN BY
Claire Welch

This edition first published in the UK in 2007
By Green Umbrella Publishing

© Green Umbrella Publishing 2007

www.greenumbrella.co.uk

Publishers: Jules Gammond and Vanessa Gardner

Printed and bound in China

ISBN: 978-1-905828-74-6

JAZZ

Legends

JAZZ

Legends

CONTENTS

CONTENTS

JAZZ *Legends*

LOUIS
ARMSTRONG

Born: 4 July 1900 in New Orleans, Louisiana
Died: 6 July 1971 in Queens, New York
Instrument: Vocals/trumpet
Suggested listening: "What A Wonderful World"
Trivia: Louis Armstrong's former home was opened to the public as a museum on 15 October 2003

Born in Storyville, one of the poorest parts of New Orleans, Louis Armstrong's background and difficult early life did little to prevent him from becoming possibly the most influential jazz musician of all time. His father was a workman while his mother was a maid and part-time prostitute.

Armstrong believed he was born on 4 July 1900 although after his death, on 6 July 1971, it was claimed that the exceptional trumpeter and singer was actually born on 4 August more than a year later. There is no conclusive evidence to support this either way. His early life involved supporting his mother and sister Beatrice, earning what he could from any kind of job he could get, including singing on street corners at night. Aged 11, after firing a gun into the air on New Year's Eve, Armstrong was sent by a juvenile court to the Jones Home for Coloured Waifs, where he joined the brass band. He tried various instruments before finally settling on the cornet. This was to mark a turning point for Armstrong.

On his release, around the age of 14, he supported himself by playing with pick-up bands in small clubs with the noted musician and Armstrong's mentor Joe "King" Oliver who, along with Jelly Roll Morton and Sidney Bechet, were creating a distinctive and popular band music mixed with blues and ragtime. Jazz was about to become a musical phenomenon.

Armstrong played on the Strekfus Mississippi river boats with Fate Marable's band and also worked with Kid Ory's band. He also played for Zutty Singleton in New Orleans and the Allen Brass Band as well as the Silver Leaf Band, but it was a telegram from his mentor "King" Oliver that made his dreams come true when he asked Armstrong to join his band in Lincoln Gardens in Chicago.

Louis Armstrong's popularity soared during the early 1920s, first in Chicago with Oliver's Creole Jazz Band and then New York, where he heavily influenced the Fletcher Henderson Orchestra with his improvisation. His "scat" singing transformed vocal tradition and when he returned to Chicago in 1926 he was famous on the radio and had appeared on numerous records. Audiences were wowed in jazz clubs with his imaginative groundbreaking trumpet solos. In February 1924 he married Lillian Hardin, a pianist and music arranger for the Creole Jazz Band, who pressured Armstrong to leave the band in search of something better. He joined Ollie Powers' Harmony Syncopators briefly before moving to New York to join the Fletcher Henderson Orchestra where he stayed for 13 months.

JAZZ *Legends*

JAZZ Legends

His return to Chicago saw him join his wife's band at the Dreamland Café and the Carrol Dickenson Orchestra. He released records under his own name for the first time and Louis Armstrong's "Hot Five" and "Hot Seven" are jazz classics which show his creative talents at their best. Armstrong continued to play in Carrol Dickenson's Orchestra until 1929 at the Sunset where he met future manager Joe Glaser. Louis Armstrong and his Stompers played the Sunset until he moved to Los Angeles in 1930 where he fronted Louis Armstrong and his Sebastian New Cotton Club Orchestra, but he returned to Chicago the following year to assemble a band for touring. During 1931 he also went back to New Orleans for the first time in nine years to work with "King" Oliver's Creole Jazz Band once again.

After separating from his wife, Armstrong spent the next three years touring the US and the UK where he was a huge success. He also visited other European countries before returning to the US to hire Joe Glaser as his manager. The partnership proved to be beneficial for Armstrong, despite rumours of Glaser's connections to Al Capone, and they remained a team as well as firm friends until Glaser's death in 1969.

Some time before this, Armstrong had become known as "Satch". It wasn't particularly a name he liked, but it was one he could live with and, following World War II and the early years of the Cold War, he was "Ambassador Satch" acting as a goodwill ambassador for the US with the support of the State Department.

His popularity remained and a 1956 concert saw 100,000 fans turn up in Ghana to mark its recent independence.

In 1963 he released the huge international hit "Hello Dolly" which eventually knocked the Beatles off the Number 1 slot and his 1968 "What A Wonderful World" summed up Armstrong's own philosophy "…see what a wonderful world it would be if only we…give it a chance. Love, baby, love. That's the secret…"

He was an inspiration to all those he knew and to all those who knew and loved his music and he did more than any other legend to influence the swing era. His death made front page news globally and more than 25,000 mourners filed past his coffin at the New York National Guard Armory.

ABOVE
Louis Armstrong in the Fifties, a time of great creativity for him.

LEFT
Louis Armstrong in concert, 1965.

COUNTBASIE

Born: 21 August 1904 in Red Bank, New Jersey
Died: 26 April 1984 in Hollywood, Florida
Instrument: Piano
Suggested listening: "One O'Clock Jump"
Trivia: Basie's collaboration with Frank Sinatra — "Sinatra-Basie" — reached Number 2 in the UK album charts in 1963

W illiam "Count" Basie is an American jazz legend who excelled on the piano and organ, which combined with his talents as a bandleader and composer, puts him among the greatest jazz musicians of all time. Basie was renowned for his contrapuntal accents on piano which characterised a "jumping" beat which became his trademark.

He was born on 21 August 1904 in Red Bank, New Jersey where his father, Harvey Lee Basie worked as a coachman for an affluent family before cars replaced horses, and his mother, Lillian Ann Childs, took in laundry while teaching her son the piano as a child. Count Basie wanted to be a drummer, but the talents of Sonny Greer (Duke Ellington's drummer between 1919-51) put him off and he concentrated on the piano. Basie went to Harlem where Fats Waller taught him informally before he began as a soloist and accompanist to blues singers in 1924. Touring with the Theater Owners Bookers Association (TOBA) took him to Kansas City in Missouri and in 1928 he joined Walter Page's Blue Devils.

In 1929, Basie joined Kansas City's Bennie Moten Band as pianist and it was at this time that he began to coin the name "Count". His own band was formed in 1934 but he soon returned to Moten's band, although the maestro's death in 1935 saw the band unsuccessful in its attempts to stay together. Again, Basie started his own band with many Moten band members, called the Count Basie Orchestra, which saw them leave Kansas City and head for Chicago.

Initially, the band was rewarded with a long contract with one of the Chicago clubs. This led to a recording session in October 1936 with producer John Hammond but the band moved to New York later that year. While playing on the radio, the band was signed with Decca Record Company who held contracts with other highly successful artists of the time. Basie's music remained defined and he developed a style of melodic leads which allowed him to lead the band from the piano while blending with the rhythm section. The success of the rhythm section was partly due to the talents of "Papa" Joe Jones who pioneered the high-hat cymbal style. The band established four-beat jazz while soloists including Harry Edison, Dicky Wells and Benny Morton ensured that the orchestra was the number one of swing.

His talents and success as a bandleader enabled him to work with some of the best musicians of the time including Lester Young, Walter Page, Buck Clayton, Freddie Green,

JAZZ *Legends*

Herschel Evans and, of course, Joe Jones. He also had access to the best music arrangers who understood his band and their abilities, including Jimmy Mundy. This brought out the best in an already superb band and Basie used this to showcase some of the biggest names in the industry including Big Joe Turner and Billie Holiday. He married Catherine Morgan and they moved to Queens, New York in 1942.

Despite the decline of the big band era, Basie's distinctive style of piano playing helped to keep jazz alive while he remained committed to the Kansas City Jazz style.

Keeping the focus on jazz meant that Count Basie's band was to become one of the most famous backing bands in history, most notably with Joe Williams on the 1956 album "Count Basie Swings, Joe Williams Sings" and the 1957 album "One O'Clock Jump". Times were tough in the 1950s and Basie was forced to reduce the full orchestra to groups of six or nine players which included the likes of Clark Terry and Buddy Rich.

Appearing as himself along with the band, Basie acted in the 1960 film, *Cinderfella* by Jerry Lewis. Lewis also used Basie's "Blues In Hoss' Flat" as a basis for a routine in his film *The Errand Boy*. Ella Fitzgerald and Basie made an electric

team which was highly regarded by critics. As the quintessential swing singer "Ella And Basie!" is remembered as one of Fitzgerald's greatest recordings. They recorded the 1979 albums "Digital III At Montreux", "A Classy Pair" and "Perfect Match" following their tour together in the mid-1970s. Basie also enjoyed a fruitful relationship with Frank Sinatra recording "Sinatra-Basie" in 1963 and "It Might As Well Be Swing" the following year, arranged by the now legendary Quincy Jones.

Before his death from pancreatic cancer on 26 April 1984 at the age of 79, Basie received one of the Kennedy Center Honours in 1981. The Count Basie Theatre in Red Bank, New Jersey was named after him and he was entered into the Long Island Music Hall of Fame in 2007 for being one of the greatest jazz musicians in history.

ABOVE
Count Basie on stage at The London Palladium, 1984.

LEFT
Count Basie at his piano, 1943.

ACKER**BILK**

Born: 28 January 1929 in Pensford, Somerset
Instrument: Clarinet
Suggested listening: "Stranger On The Shore"
Trivia: Acker Bilk – with his trademark goatee beard, bowler hat and striped waistcoat – quipped that "Stranger On The Shore" was his old-age pension

Presented with an MBE for services to music on 1 January 2001 and an entry in Who's Who in 2004, the British icon of jazz, Acker Bilk, also received a BBC Jazz Award in 2005 and an honorary MA from the University of Bristol.

Born Bernard Stanley Bilk on 28 January 1929 in Pensford, Somerset, his name quickly changed to Acker (the Somerset slang for mate/friend) which is apt for the man who is described as a "Great Master of the Clarinet". Acker Bilk's parents were keen for him to learn the piano, but this restricted his love of outdoor activities such as football. During a school fight he lost two front teeth while a sledging accident cost him half a finger. It is these two accidents which may have led to his unique style which has seen him become a renowned figure in the world of jazz with his trademark bowler, goatee and striped waistcoat.

Acker Bilk has been arguably one of the world's greatest clarinettists since the late 1950s with a rich vibrato style of playing. Before turning to music as a career, Bilk worked for the Bristol Wills Tobacco factory and had an interest in boxing. He married his childhood sweetheart, Jean, and had two children, Peter and Jenny.

In 1948, he began playing the clarinet, borrowing a military clarinet so he could copy records while he was in the Royal Engineers. He was severely disciplined when caught sleeping on duty and practised the clarinet to combat boredom when he was sent to the glasshouse. After being demobbed, Acker Bilk formed his own band, but moved to London in 1951 so that he could join Ken Colyer's band.

In 1956 he again started his own band and in 1960 "Summer Set" – a pun on Somerset – was released in the UK charts which led to 11 Top 59 hit singles and another album, "Creole Jazz". It wasn't until two years later that Acker Bilk became an international star when he wrote and performed "Stranger On The Shore". Originally entitled "Jenny" after his daughter, the title was changed after the BBC wanted to use the tune as the theme to a popular UK television show. He recorded the piece as the title track to a new album which was backed by the Leon Young String Chorale. This experiment became his keynote piece and shot to Number 1 in the US as well as the UK. It was at this time that Acker Bilk's PR team were known as the Bilk Marketing Board (another pun: this time on the then Milk Marketing Board in the UK).

Bilk's first big break had come after his move to London when the band was contracted to play for six weeks at a bar in Dusseldorf. This concentration helped the band to musically discipline itself.

JAZZ *Legends*

JAZZ*Legends*

His subsequent albums were successfully released on both sides of the Atlantic including a successful collaboration with Bent Fabric, the Danish jazz pianist and composer. The US subsidiary of Atlantic Records, Atco, released the album "The Alley Cat" in the States but success waned when rock and roll made a huge impact on the international scene at the beginning of 1964.

Undeterred, Bilk changed direction and went back to performing live. "Aria" went to Number 5 in the UK charts in 1976 and there was more recognition when "Stranger On The Shore" was used for the film *Sweet Dreams* about the life of country music legend Patsy Cline.

Acker Bilk, despite being in his 70s, still loves playing with his Paramount Jazz Band and string ensembles where his talents with rich sound and romantic melodies prevail. In 2001 and 2002, Bilk recorded his "Evening Shadows" and "Summer Set" with Van Morrison which were released with lyrics by Van Morrison in 2003.

A year later, Acker Bilk released his first live album for 10 years with the Paramount Jazz Band, "As Time Goes By" with band members Enrico Tomasso, Ian Bateman, Malcom Creese, Richie Bryant and Colin Wood. The album was produced by Acker's tour manager of 30 years, Les Squires.

Acker Bilk and his wife have now moved back to Pensford in Somerset where he enjoys a love of painting. Perhaps this is fitting for a man who toured the world for more than 50 years – the Australians are keen for him to return – although he is still active with the Paramount Jazz Band. Despite his still heavy schedule, Acker Bilk, finds time to support various charities, notably campaigning for recognition of the men and women who died serving in the Suez Crisis – something that's personal to Acker and close to his heart and which he achieved in 2003 – as well as cancer charities.

Acker was diagnosed with throat cancer in 1999 and underwent radiotherapy. His painting helped him through this difficult time. As a serious and dedicated jazz legend, Acker Bilk is often attributed with being the originator of "Hyung-Tiger" playing, copied by artists such as Ted Morton.

ABOVE
Acker Bilk perfoms at The London Palladium.

LEFT
Acker Bilk with two members of his Paramount Jazz Band.

JAZZ *Legends*

JOHN
COLTRANE

Born: 23 September 1926 in Hamlet, North Carolina
Died: 17 July 1967 in Long Island, New York
Instrument: Saxophone
Suggested listening: "A Love Supreme"
Trivia: John Coltrane's son Ravi is also a well-respected saxophonist

Nicknamed Trane, John William Coltrane was born in Hamlet, North Carolina on 23 September 1926. Trane went on to become a hugely influential jazz musician with recordings from as early as 1946, although his recording career did not really take off until 1955. Trane was identified as reshaping modern jazz and the jazz expectations of the saxophone while being a huge influence on generations of saxophonists that followed him. Also hailed for his compositions, from 1957 he recorded and produced literally dozens of albums – although many were not actually released until years after his death.

During a time of American racial segregation, Trane grew up at his grandfather's home in High Point in an extended family which was quite privileged. But all that changed when the loss of four family members, including Trane's grandfather, forced his mother and aunt into domestic service and the family to the brink of poverty.

Not surprisingly this young talented musician began practicing obsessively. He was exposed to the European canon, which heavily influenced his later music, and the concept of jazz through the radio, movies and jukeboxes. Having started with the clarinet, Trane switched to the alto sax and when he was drafted into the Navy in 1945 he joined the band. Several recordings have survived from this period in his life. Charlie Parker was Trane's biggest influence, along with Miles Davis, and he eventually joined Dizzy Gillespie's big band in 1949.

He switched to tenor saxophone after the big band's break-up in 1950, but returned to Philadelphia in 1951. After brief spells with Earl Bostic's band and Eddie "Cleanhead" Vinson, he joined Johnny Hodges who was on a sabbatical from the Duke Ellington Orchestra. By the summer of 1955, Trane was freelancing in Philadelphia. Miles Davis was looking to form a quintet and Trane jumped at the chance to be part of Miles's "First Great Quintet" which gave him the opportunity to showcase his ability, particularly on two influential recordings for Prestige in 1956.

But he came in for some criticism with his playing which was described by some as "angry and harsh". Harry Frost was particularly harsh and even went so far as to comment that his solos were: "Extended double-time flurries notable for their lack of direction." Perhaps such critique encouraged Trane to clean up his act as in 1957 he had kicked his addiction to heroin and once again began to practice obsessively, just as he had done during his youth. He began to develop his compositions more fully and teamed up with Thelonious Monk at the Five Spot Café in New York for a six-month contract.

JAZZ *Legends*

JAZZ *Legends*

But the following year he was back with Miles Davis, in his, by now, sextet including Cannonball Adderley, Wynton Kelly, Paul Chambers, Philly Joe Jones, Jimmy Cobb, Red Garland and Bill Evans, where he stayed until 1960.

During his time with Miles Davis, Trane recorded his own sessions including "Giant Steps" for Atlantic Records with its complex and difficult chord progressions. He also swapped to soprano sax – almost completely unheard of in jazz music at the time. The soprano gave him the opportunity to reach much higher registers and enabled faster play, although it may have been due to the acute pain in his gums from playing tenor sax that prompted the switch.

He formed his own band in 1960 which comprised Elvin Jones, drummer, McCoy Tyner, piano and Steve Davis on bass. The band recorded "My Favourite Things" for Atlantic Records with whom Trane, playing soprano sax, had already signed a contract. He then recorded "Ole Coltrane" before signing with Impulse! giving him once again the chance to work with engineer Rudy Van Gelder (who previously recorded Trane's sessions with Prestige).

During the early 1960s, Trane altered his style which drew some fierce criticism from some quarters, including an accusation from one magazine that he was anti-jazz. He was also famously booed off stage at a gig in France and audiences everywhere were perplexed at his shift in style. Meanwhile, Trane's "Classic Quartet" moved towards a static harmony which gave him room to expand his improvisation – harmonies were still complex – but by now Trane just wanted to rework his previous music. His albums became more accessible for listeners and he began a collaboration with Duke Ellington.

"A Love Supreme" was recorded in 1964 with the "Classic Quartet" which turned out to be their most famous record. Trane's interest in the spiritual would become a major influence in his work along with avant-garde jazz while he was instrumental in Impulse! becoming a free jazz record label. He was also heavily influenced by Ayler during his later years and the abrasive playing style of saxophonist Pharoah Sanders who joined the band in 1965.

Trane himself was becoming more dissonant and his atonal improvisations were often accompanied with over-blowing to make an emotional exclamation mark. His influence in jazz music is legendary, but he also interested the new musical genre – rock – through the likes of Jimi Hendrix and the Stooges. He died on 17 July 1967.

JAZZ*Legends*

JAMIE
CULLUM

Born: 20 August 1979 in Romford, Essex
Instrument: Vocals/piano/guitar
Suggested listening: "Photograph"
Trivia: Jamie Cullum gave a masterclass to the students of BBC1's Comic Relief Does Fame Academy reality show in March 2007

The jazz pianist and singer/songwriter Jamie Cullum cites his paternal grandmother Omi (a Jewish refugee from Prussia) as his "cultural icon". Born in Essex on 20 August 1979, he was brought up in Hullavington in Wiltshire. His first album "Jamie Cullum Trio – Heard It All Before" was released in 1999 and only 500 copies were made (some of which later went on to sell for up to £600).

The success of this album resulted in his appearing on "Songs Of The Summer", an album by Geoff Gascoyne, before embarking on his second album "Pointless Nostalgic" in 2001 shortly after graduating with a first in English from the University of Reading. While reading English, Cullum was keen to further his musical talents and took jobs as a singer and pianist anywhere he could get a gig. His early musical influences include Miles Davis and Herbie Hancock as well as Steely Dan, rock, blues and hip hop.

His third album "Twentysomething" was released in October 2003 by Universal Classics & Jazz – the label he signed with earlier that year – and went platinum, becoming the number one best selling studio album by a jazz musician in the UK. This success is made more impressive by the fact that Cullum is completely self-taught and although he is primarily concerned with jazz he is also renowned for his pop abilities. His musical involvement has ranged from drumming in a hip hop group to playing guitar in rock bands but jazz is undeniably where his heart is as a top performer.

He wrote the music together with his brother Ben for the West End stage production of *When Harry Met Sally*. Ben has been one of Cullum's biggest musical influences along with the stompbox. Cullum was exposed to the stompbox while visiting Australia. A small wooden block, it is used to amplify a tapping foot, which Cullum uses to great effect during his unique entertainment style to enhance upbeat and fast-paced songs. Another of his unique styles is the use of a looping machine and beatboxing. Fans of Cullum agree that his gigs are a completely different experience, offering something out of the ordinary. Exciting and upbeat combined with Cullum's amazing charisma, his gigs are an experience to remember where set lists are a thing of the past and he plays what he feels like at the time.

In July 2003, Cullum received the Rising Star Award at the British Jazz Awards ceremony and the following year was nominated for the British Breakthrough Act at the Brit Awards. He and peer Katie Mellua performed the Cure's "Love Cats" at the ceremony. In 2005 he was again nominated at the Brits, this time for two awards, Best Male Artist

and Best Live Act, but it was his Grammy award and BBC Radio 2's Artist of the Year award presented at the BBC Jazz Awards that highlighted his extraordinary career.

Although Cullum has been known to cover artists such as the White Stripes, Elton John, Gnarls Barkley and Massive Attack, his third album "Catching Tales" was original work by both Cullum and his older brother Ben. The album also features singer/songwriter Ed Harcourt who also collaborated with Cullum on one of his own favourite songs "Back To The Ground".

Released in 2005, the album includes "Fascinating Rhythm" on the European version (not France) while it doesn't on the US edition. "Mind Trick" was the next single to be released in the UK written by the Cullum brothers, while the third track to be released – "Photograph" – was written by Jamie Cullum. "Catching Tales" is also one of those rare albums these days to be released on double vinyl.

A collaboration with Pharrell Williams, the American singer, rapper and producer, "Catching Tales" was to feature the track "Wifey", but publishing laws prevented it and the American R&B singer Usher released the song on Pharrell Williams' album. Ben Cullum plays bass throughout the album while Ed Harcourt remains an inspiration to Cullum who is aiming to work with the musician again in the future.

From October 2005 to December 2006 Cullum went on tour with "Catching Tales" including gigs in Europe, Asia, South Africa, New Zealand and four visits to the US. As a dynamic musician, Cullum is supported by his band with bassist Geoff Gascoyne, Sebastiaan De Krom on drums, Tom Richards on sax and Rory Simmons on trumpet and guitar. The album "Live At Ronnie Scott's" was released in 2006.

2007 will be a quiet year for his avid fans as Cullum takes time to write music and record a new album as well as continuing to work with his brother Ben. He may even have time to enjoy Swindon Town's matches – this young jazz legend knows all about being an avid fan himself.

ABOVE
Jamie Cullum – away from his piano.

LEFT
Jamie performing at Arrow Jazz in the Park, 2006.

MILES DAVIS

Born: 26 May 1926 in Alton, Illinois

Died: 28 September 1991 in New York

Instrument: Trumpet

Suggested listening: "Milestones"

Trivia: Rolling Stone magazine ranked Davis at number 88 on their list of the 100 Greatest Artists of All Time in 2004

One of the most distinguished jazz musicians of all time has to be Miles Dewey Davis III who was born on 26 May 1926 into an affluent American family in Illinois. A year later the family moved to St Louis and Davis learned to ride horses at a young age on the family's extensive ranch. His mother, a blues pianist, kept her talents hidden from her son as she felt that black music was not genteel enough for him. Instead, she wanted him to learn the violin.

However, he took up the trumpet aged nine under direction from Elwood Buchanan, although he didn't seriously learn to play until he was 13. Buchanan was instrumental in keeping Davis's vibrato to a minimum and this gave the young musician a clear tone which he would establish and maintain throughout his musical career.

As a friend of Davis, Clark Terry was another important influence on his early life. By 16 he was a member of the Musicians Union (MU) and worked professionally outside of his schooling. He played for a year in the Blue Devils under Eddie Randle, and Sonny Stitt was anxious for him to join Tiny Bradshaw although his mother had the final say and he finished his final year at school.

Billy Eckstine visited St Louis with his band in 1944 and Davis joined Dizzy Gillespie and Charlie Parker along with other members of the band for two weeks when Buddy Anderson was struck down by illness. That same year the budding musician won a scholarship to the Julliard in New York, but he neglected his studies in order to track down Charlie Parker. He made his first recording the following year and was soon a member of Parker's quintet.

Davis's distinctive trumpet style was already established but he lacked confidence as a soloist and sometimes stumbled over notes showing a lack of virtuosity. After three years, in 1948, Davis was beginning to blossom and his own recording career began to take off. He worked with the unusual combination of a French horn and tuba in a nonet and was eventually signed by Capitol Records. It was around this time that his collaboration with Gil Evans began – a partnership that would last more than 20 years – and he made his first visit to Paris where he performed in the Jazz Festival.

From 1950 for the next five years, like many other contemporaries, Davis recorded on the Prestige and Blue Note labels where he worked with John Lewis, Kenny Clarke, Art Blakey, Horace Silver, Thelonious Monk and Charles Mingus to name but a few. Ahmad Jamal, the pianist, was also an influence on Davis at this time. But, New York jazz clubs

JAZZ *Legends*

were prone to easy drug taking and Davis developed a heroin addiction. The effect on his musical ability was immense and he was more than aware of this. He returned to St Louis and locked himself in a room at the ranch for seven days until the drug was out of his system. This clean-up led to some influential recordings for Prestige in 1954 and the use of his muted trumpet which was to remain a trademark for Davis for the rest of his career.

Davis's revival came in the form of a solo at the Newport Jazz Festival on Thelonious Monk's "Round Midnight". Davis was popular again and signed for Columbia. He set up the Miles Davis Quintet featuring John Coltrane, Red Garland, Paul Chambers and Philly Joe Jones with its bebop style while Davis experimented with modal music. This prolific line up of jazz greats caused some criticism at the time although the quintet is widely regarded as one of the best jazz ensembles of all time. Due to heroin use by other members the band was disbanded in 1957 and Davis visited France to work on a soundtrack for Louis Malle but a year later was back to reform his quintet as a sextet with Julian "Cannonball" Adderley on alto sax. The band recorded "Milestones" which aptly reflected the past and future of jazz at the time.

Gil Evans was a talented arranger and his work with Davis showed off both their exceptional talents. In 1958 the album "Porgy And Bess" became one of Davis's own favourites while "The Maids Of Cadiz" was the first classical music he recorded. "Sketches Of Spain" in 1960 featured work by the legendary classical composer Joaquin Rodrigo and "Miles Davis At Carnegie Hall" the following year included another work by Rodrigo "Concierto de Aranjuez".

Davis can arguably be attributed with being at the forefront of jazz and its developments from the end of World War II to the early 1990s. He was an innovator and leader whose many recordings and live performances often featured major figures from the world of jazz. After his death on 28 September 1991, Miles Davis was entered in the Rock and Roll Hall of Fame, the St Louis Walk of Fame and the Big Band and Jazz Hall of Fame.

ABOVE
Miles Davis in 1991 – the year he passed away.

LEFT
Miles Davis playing the trumpet, 1955.

JAZZ*Legends*

DUKE**ELLINGTON**

Born: 29 April 1899 in Washington DC
Died: 24 May 1974 in New York
Instrument: Piano
Suggested listening: "Skin Deep"
Trivia: Both Judy Collins ("Song For Duke" in 1975) and Stevie Wonder ("Sir Duke" in 1977) have recorded their own tributes to Duke Ellington

E dward Kennedy "Duke" Ellington was reluctant to use the term jazz and preferred to call what he did "music", although many would disagree with this great man and argue that he was one of the most important figures in the world of jazz to ever emerge.

Born on 29 April 1899 in Washington DC, Duke was raised by his mother and his father – (the son of a former slave) who made blueprints for the US Navy and worked as a butler at the White House. Both Duke's parents were pianists so it is not surprising that this jazz legend became one of the world's most prolific jazz pianists, composer and band leader. He wasn't keen on piano lessons to start with, but by the age of 14 he began to take his studies seriously.

At 17, Duke was playing professionally and studied commercial art at the Armstrong Manual Training School. His studies were never finished and he left before graduating to pursue his love of music. In 1923 he formed the Washingtonians, a small dance band, which moved to New York where they took up residence at the Club Kentucky. Four years later Ellington was approached by the Harlem Cotton Club to become the house band when "King" Oliver turned the opportunity down. Ellington quickly accepted and with a weekly radio broadcast and famous clientele he was set on the road to stardom.

His rise to critical acclaim was helped by many band members who would themselves later go on to become famous. Bubber Miley on trumpet was instrumental in changing the band's rigid style for a more "New Orleans" or "jungle" approach while Johnny Hodges – who joined the orchestra in 1928 – was undoubtedly the band's leading soloist. Famous for his crooning ballads on alto sax, Hodges remained with the band until his death in 1970. Then for 12 years Barney Bigard was a master of the New Orleans style of jazz on the clarinet while Harry Carney on baritone sax was the longest lasting member of the band from 1927-74. Other members of the band included drummer Sonny Greer, Fred Guy, Lawrence Brown and Joe "Tricky Sam" Nanton.

Irving Mills, Duke's manager, was largely responsible for his popularity during the 1930s, but the arrangement came to an end in 1937. The band's popularity was huge among the black and white communities despite continued racial segregation, and they enjoyed a huge following in the UK and Europe.

During the 1940s it was band members Jimmy Blanton and Ben Webster who were to add creativity to the music and Ray Nance joined the band bringing the violin to the mix.

JAZZ*Legends*

Some of the most memorable music from this time includes "Cottontail", "Mainstream" and "Streets Of New York". These three-minute masterpieces all came from Ellington, his son Mercer, Billy Strayhorn and various other members. Ellington's aim was to extend this form and although recorded in 1931, "Creole Rhapsody" now came into its own. But, on the other hand, Ellington's longer musical works were not well received and, coupled with the development of modern jazz and a shift towards vocalists such as Frank Sinatra, Duke's position became threatened.

In 1951, significant band members left to pursue other ideas and within four years Ellington found himself without a recording contract. Undeterred, Duke appeared at the Newport Jazz Festival in 1956 and "Diminuendo And Crescendo In Blue" with Paul Gonsalves on sax who garnered much needed attention. Ella Fitzgerald recorded the "Duke Ellington Songbook" in the late 1950s while the early 1960s saw him recording with Charlie Mingus and John Coltrane. Touring all over the world now took up time and he started new collaborations with other musicians.

Duke also contributed serious work to both film and theatre. His debut came with the short film *Black And Tan* in 1929 and he appeared in *Check and Double Check* which became a huge hit and did much to promote Duke Ellington. The 1930s and 1940s saw Ellington and his band in many films including *Murder At The Vanities* in 1934. The 1950s saw Ellington working on the scores for film soundtracks such as *Anatomy Of A Murder* (1959) starring James Stewart and *Paris Blues* (1961) starring Sidney Poitier and Paul Newman playing jazz musicians.

His later music is dominated by his style of the 1940s, although he never lost his creativity, and three concerts aimed at fusing Christian liturgy with jazz took place during the late 1960s and early 1970s. Ellington was awarded with the Presidential Medal of Freedom in 1969, the Legion of Honor (France 1973) although he was turned down for a Pulitzer Prize in 1965. Duke Ellington died of lung cancer in May 1974.

LEFT
Duke Ellington in concert, 1963.

BELOW
Duke Ellington, one of the most influential figures in jazz, 1972.

JAZZ *Legends*

ELLA
FITZGERALD

Born: 25 April 1917 in Newport News, Virginia

Died: 15 June 1996 in Beverley Hills, Los Angeles

Instrument: Vocals

Suggested listening: "A-Tisket, A-Tasket"

Trivia: While on tour in Dallas, everyone in Ella's dressing room was arrested for shooting dice but the police still had the nerve to ask for autographs

K nown as "The First Lady of Song", Ella Jane Fitzgerald was born on 25 April 1917 in Newport News, Virginia, in the US. This great lady of jazz was a legend the world over and brought together people from all walks of life who had a common bond – the love of Ella Fitzgerald. Fitzgerald worked with some of the best including Nat King Cole, Duke Ellington, Frank Sinatra, Dizzie Gillespie and Count Basie to name but a few. Renowned for sultry ballads and sweet jazz, Fitzgerald set the stage at the world's top venues with her diverse vocal range.

Her parents separated when Fitzgerald was young she moved with her mother to Yonkers in New York where they lived with Joseph Da Silva. Her half-sister, Frances, was born in 1923 and Fitzgerald worked odd jobs to help the family. Fitzgerald was a popular child and made friends easily in her mixed-raced neighbourhood where she liked to be considered a tomboy. Life was to have its blows and in 1932, her mother died from injuries she sustained in a car crash. The loss hit the young singer hard and she eventually returned to her mother's family in Virginia. Not long after, Da Silva died from a heart attack and Frances joined her. Fitzgerald spiralled into depression and endured an unhappy period in her life. Things further declined when the 15-year-old found herself in trouble and was taken into custody. Fitzgerald spent time in a reform school where she was regularly beaten She escaped, only to find herself living alone and without money during the Great Depression which had gripped the US.

Two years later saw Fitzgerald perform at the Apollo Theatre on Amateur Night where she sang "Judy" by Hoagy Carmichael, and Fitzgerald knew that singing was in her heart and soul. A spot with Chick Webb's band for $12.50 a set Fitzgerald on the road to stardom. Her first recording "Love And Kisses" was released in 1936 on Decca at the same time that she was performing at the Harlem's Savoy Ballroom with Webb's band. Also at this time Fitzgerald was gaining a reputation as a forerunning bebop singer where her talents for using her voice to imitate any instrument in the band were second to none. She began experimenting with scat singing and throughout her life was to thrill and impress her audiences with her expert improvisations and vocalisations. Scat singing – under Fitzgerald – became an art form.

Her success and popularity grew and in 1946 Fitzgerald married her second husband, bassist Ray Brown,. The couple adopted a son, Ray Junior. With husband Ray working for Norman Granz on the "Jazz at the Philharmonic" tour, Fitzgerald was soon involved in

JAZZ *Legends*

the event. Granz recognised her star quality and knew she was destined for great things. The relationship was to prove the start of a lifelong business partnership and friendship.

Ira Gershwin is known to have remarked: "I never knew how good our songs were until I heard Ella Fitzgerald sing them". This great legend of jazz was to have the same effect on every audience she sang to and she began to appear on a number of television variety shows including The Bing Crosby Show, *The Ed Sullivan Show* and *The Tonight Show*. She was a huge success and quickly became a popular favourite on the small screen.

Work pressure saw Fitzgerald and Brown divorce in 1952 although the couple remained good friends and while gruelling schedules meant that Ray Jr felt his relationship with his parents could have been better, Fitzgerald is known to have loved him unconditionally. Despite family problems, the singer's professional career was unstoppable and she even played the Mocambo nightclub with Marilyn Monroe in the front every night during the 1950s at the superstar's request. The result was that Fitzgerald never played a small jazz club again and with her hard work and determination began touring all over the world.

Fitzgerald's exceptional talents saw her inducted into the Down Beat Magazine Hall of Fame in 1974 while President Ronald Reagan presented her with the National Medal of Arts in 1987. She also received a star on the Hollywood Walk of Fame.

Even ill health including a coronary bypass and diabetes did not stop the lady of jazz. The late 1980s saw this incredible woman return to the stage and by the 1990s Fitzgerald had recorded more than 200 albums. Her final concert was at the famous Carnegie Hall in New York in 1991. However, her health was to suffer further and both her legs were amputated below her knees as a result of her worsening diabetes. Life ended for this inspiring woman on 15 June 1996 but her timeless voice is still enjoyed by her fans today.

ABOVE
Ella chats to her pianist, 1948.

LEFT
Ella at Ronnie Scott's Jazz Club in 1973.

DIZZY**GILLESPIE**

Born: 21 October 1917 in Cheraw, South Carolina
Died: 6 January 1993 in New York
Instrument: Trumpet
Suggested listening: "Kerouac"
Trivia: Dizzy Gillespie was due to play at Carnegie Hall for the 33rd time on 26 November 1992 but was too ill to perform

J ohn Birks "Dizzy" Gillespie is undoubtedly one of the greatest jazz trumpeters of the 20th century and one of the pioneers of bebop as well as a singer, band leader and composer. As an accomplished composer and arranger, Gillespie wrote some of the greatest jazz classics of the era including "Groovin' High" and "Manteca".

Born in Cheraw, South Carolina on 21 October 1917, he was the youngest of 10 children. Gillespie's father was a musician and band leader but he died when his son was 10 years old, never hearing him play the trumpet. Gillespie had originally liked the trombone, but with arms too short to play the instrument well, he was encouraged by the recordings of legend Louis Armstrong, and not Roy Eldridge as previously thought, making the trumpet his second choice.

Teaching himself the trumpet at the age of 13, he won a music scholarship to the Laurinburg Institute in North Carolina where he stayed for two years. But he dropped out of school during the Depression and worked in the cotton fields in order to help support his family. Gillespie's family moved to Philadelphia in 1935 and he began playing with local bands. It was here that he picked up his nickname "Dizzy". Some say this was because he was dizzy like a fox with his crazy antics on stage.

He played with Frankie Fairfax at first before learning the solos of Roy Eldridge, whom he replaced in Teddy Hill's band in 1937 when he moved to New York. Three years later, Gillespie met Charlie Parker, another jazz great who together with Gillespie did more than any other musician to develop modern jazz and the bebop style they became so famous for. It was also the year that he made his first record.

During this time, Gillespie also played occasionally with the Savoy Sultans and the Chick Webb Orchestra. But, his lack of experience also resulted in him being left out of a recording in Paris with Teddy Hills while his popularity within the band plummeted due to his money lending schemes. It was in the summer of 1939 that he joined Cab Calloway's band and became renowned for being a trumpet soloist – he went on to record "Kerouac" in 1941 which was part of the bebop revolution. Bebop in a pure form only lasted a number of years and it was the easier listening lighter bebop which made the music accessible to audiences that made Gillespie popular.

Gillespie and Parker were regulars at jamming sessions at the Minton Playhouse and Monroe's Uptown House where music like "A Night In Tunisia" and "Anthropology" was composed. These were radically different from the jazz of before both in harmony and

JAZZ*Legends*

rhythm and the two men set up a quintet. Around this time Gillespie is also attributed with teaching this new style to many of the then future greats including Miles Davis and Max Roach.

However, the audience at a gig in Billy Berg's club in Los Angeles was confused by the new style and it led to the band's break-up. Gillespie was desperate to lead a big band while Parker was content with a small group and the occasional big band gig. The late 1940s saw another shift in style for Gillespie who was influenced by Mario Bauza who introduced him to Afro-Cuban music. When someone fell on his trumpet in 1953, Gillespie found that he preferred the 45-degree angle of the bell.

He appeared as a soloist many times for Norman Granzs Jazz at the Philharmonic and started a number of small bands himself, but it was not until he visited France in 1952 that he proved himself as a big band leader. He had been invited to play at Salon du Jazz by Charles Delaunay but with no other work commitments found time to record in the Theatre des Champs-Elysees and embark on his Blue Star sessions. He returned to the US in 1953 and three years later put a band together for a State Department tour of the Middle East. He also put himself forward as a presidential candidate in 1964.

During the 1980s, Gillespie led the United Nations Orchestra while in 1989 he was crowned a traditional chief in Nigeria and received the prestigious Commandre d'Order des Artes et Lettres in France. He received 14 honorary doctorates, the Kennedy Centre Honors Award and the Duke Ellington Award.

Dizzy Gillespie died of pancreatic cancer on 6 January 1993 and was survived by his widow Lorraine, his wife of more than 50 years, and his daughter, jazz singer, Jeanie Bryson. His original trumpet, a King Silver Flair, is on display at the Smithsonian Institute in Washington DC.

DAVID

BENNYGOODMAN

Born: 30 May 1909 in Chicago, Illinois
Died: 13 June 1986 in New York
Instrument: Clarinet
Suggested listening: "And The Angels Sing"
Trivia: Benny Goodman was honoured with the Grammy Lifetime Achievement Award in 1986

Known as the "King of Swing", Benjamin David Goodman was the ninth of 12 children born to Jewish immigrants from Hungary in Chicago on 30 May 1909. His interest in jazz grew from an early age and he found himself surrounded by jazz legends such as Louis Armstrong, "Jelly Roll" Morton, Sidney Bechet and "King" Oliver during the 1920s.

Although only 10 when Goodman first tried the clarinet, he received some training from the Kehelah Jacob Synagogue before joining the Boys' Club band at Jane Addams's Hull House. He also had lessons with classical clarinettist Franz Schoepp, quickly learned to do Ted Lewis imitations and was also influenced by Johnny Dodds, Leon Roppolo, Jimmy Noone, Buster Bailey, Barney Bigard and Albert Nicholas. Goodman joined the Musicians' Union in 1923 and made regular appearances with Murph Podalasky and Jules Herbevaux. He joined the Ben Pollack Orchestra in 1925 and went on to make his first recordings in 1926. He had been heavily influenced by this time by Bix Beiderbecke especially with his on the beat attacks and his two recordings in 1928, namely "A Jazz Holiday" and "Blue" both demonstrate Beiderbecke's influence.

Goodman remained with the Ben Pollack Orchestra until 1929 but was also known to work with Meyer Davis, Sam Lanin and Nat Shilkret. Until 1934 he went freelance as a session musician working on radio and recordings for Red Nichols, Ben Selvin and Paul Whiteman among others while in 1932 he formed his own band.

With a slot on NBC's Let's Dance every week for which he used jazz charts purchased from Fletcher Henderson – as advised by agent John Hammond – and a hardworking band, Goodman's popularity soared during the mid-1930s. When the show folded, the band set off on a tour of the US, but by mid-1935 the band were disillusioned. At the final gig at the Palomar Ballroom in Los Angeles the initial response to the band was ambivalent.

Undeterred and with advice from Gene Krupa the band began to play the Henderson charts and other big swing songs. The audience response was overwhelming and subsequent audiences began a new dance and started a new craze with the "Jitterbug". This new craze backed by the ecstatic response that Goodman and his band received catapulted Goodman nationally through newspaper articles about the new phenomenon which became known as "Swing". The Benny Goodman trio with Teddy Wilson and Gene Krupa became a quartet in 1936 when Lionel Hampton joined the band.

Also at this time Goodman became famous for his classical repertoire and in 1935 performed the Clarinet Quintet by Mozart and three years later went on to perform the

JAZZ*Legends*

JAZZ*Legends*

work with the Budapest String Quartet. In January 1938, Goodman and the band were due to play at Carnegie Hall in New York. Bearing in mind that the Hall was used to classical concerts supported by high society, Goodman was rightly anxious about a "hot" band making an appearance. But the release of his movie *Hollywood Hotel* dispelled his doubts and the concert was a sell-out weeks before the event. The sets with the Count Basie and Duke Ellington bands did not go as well as expected and the audience gave a somewhat tepid response but some later sets by smaller groups and a Martha Tilton rendition of "Loch Lomond" received a much warmer response. One highlight of the evening was Goodman's band playing "Sing, Sing, Sing", but the crowning glory was Goodman finishing his solo leading in pianist Jess Stacy. The move was completely unexpected by Stacy who played four choruses in a quiet church-like style that has since become one of the most famous jazz solos ever played. The concert was particularly significant in that it brought jazz to the mainstream musical arena.

Goodman gave his first classical recital at the Town Hall in New York and later commissioned concertos from both Bela Bartok and Paul Hindemith. He appeared with many leading US orchestras performing works by Leonard Bernstein, Claude Debussy, Carl Nielsen, Poulenc, Stravinsky and Carl Maria von Weber.

Goodman was arguably the most technically prolific jazz clarinettist of all time with his virtuoso style of play. Certainly, during his lifetime there was no peer to match him. An innovator who possessed determination combined with perfection, Goodman did much to bring black music to a white audience. He was also responsible for helping to bring down the barrier of racial segregation. Black and white musicians were not permitted to play together in most clubs but Goodman broke the mould when he asked Teddy Wilson, Gene Krupa and Lionel Hampton to join the band touring only in the Northern States (his band would have been subject to arrest in the Southern States).

Goodman died on 13 June 1986 in New York, leaving behind a legacy which would influence both jazz and classical clarinettists that followed.

JAZZ*Legends*

HERBIE HANCOCK

Born: 12 April 1940 in Chicago, Illinois
Instrument: Piano/keyboards
Suggested listening: "Rockit"
Trivia: In the early 1980s, Herbie Hancock was one of the first musicians to use an Apple computer to create his music

A s an Academy Award winner, multiple Grammy Award winner and one of the most influential jazz pianists and composers from the US, Herbert Jeffrey Hancock has done it all. Born in Chicago on 12 April 1940, Herbie's career began with a classical music education where his enormous talent was recognised aged 11 when he played the first movement of Mozart's "Piano Concerto No 5 in D major" accompanied by the Chicago Symphony Orchestra.

Jazz inspired him when he was exposed to recordings of Oscar Peterson and George Shearing while notable pianists to influence him include Wynton Kelly and Bill Evans. Other jazz greats of whom he took notice were Miles Davis and John Coltrane. Hancock studied musical composition and received a double major in music and electrical engineering (which would later form the basis for his experimentation in electronic jazz fusion) from Grinnell College in 1961 and went on to gain a degree from the Manhattan School of Music.

Hancock was first hired by Donald Byrd (while still at college) and as his reputation grew he played on sessions with Oliver Nelson and Phil Woods, recording his first solo album "Takin' Off" for Blue Note in 1962. This original material was encouraged by Alfred Lions of Blue Note Records who had been more than impressed with Hancock's compositional abilities. This made the album Blue Note's first debut album with all original compositions. Miles Davis was keen to have Hancock in the new band he was assembling, but first, Hancock joined Michael Malis's quintet. This second "great quintet" was where Hancock excelled and often used chords rarely used in jazz before. Hancock's two albums of 1964 and 1965 namely "Empyrean Isles" and "Maiden Voyage" were to become two of the most prolific of the decade and were widely regarded as the foundations of the post-bop style.

The 1960s also saw Hancock working with Miles Davis and his quintet which included a line-up of saxophonist Wayne Shorter, bassist Ron Carter and Tony Williams on drums. Each member of the band somehow pushed the others musically and in short the quintet became one of the most enduring and influential ensembles in the history of jazz.

Hancock switched labels from Blue Note to Warner Brothers Records while his music of the late 1960s and early 1970s remained just as adventurous as his previous compositions and – following a lead from Davis – began experimenting with electronic instruments which formed the foundations for his jazz fusion which was to come later. He

JAZZ*Legends*

experimented with the electric piano and became a premier electric keyboard player in jazz along with Joe Zawinul and Chick Corea.

Hancock's fusion ensemble Mwandishi recorded two albums with Warner Brothers and one for Columbia Records when Hancock switched labels yet again. "Sextant" received poor sales and the group was disbanded although Hancock was already forming another ensemble, Headhunters, which was inspired by his study of Buddhism and his love of R&B music. Hancock wrote "Chameleon" for Headhunters which was a Hancock fusion classic.

The first album by the new ensemble titled "Head Hunters" was widely received in 1973 and became a major hit. A second album, "Thrust" was released in 1974 and also provoked critical acclaim. Then the Headhunters made a further successful album, "Survival Of The Fittest", but this time without Hancock.

Throughout the late 1970s and early 1980s he toured with his VSOP quintet which included all the original members from Davis's quintet except the great man himself who was replaced by Freddie Hubbard. Many of Hancock's other works and recordings of this time were only released in Japan (although some have now been re-released in the West). During the early 1980s he also concentrated on more traditional jazz and commercially-viable projects.

When Miles Davis died in 1991, Hancock, Ron Carter, Tony Williams, Wayne Shorter and Wallace Roney recorded "A Tribute To Miles" released in 1994. The album won a Grammy. "Dis Is Da Drum", also released in 1994, was Hancock's return to Acid jazz while his 1997 album with Wayne Shorter "1 + 1" featured "Aung San Suu Kyi" which won a Grammy for Best Instrumental Composition. It was "Gershwin's World" in 1998 that was to provide Hancock with great success which included George and Ira Gershwin readings, Hancock's own music and guest appearances from stars such as Stevie Wonder and Joni Mitchell.

He recorded "Future2Future" in 2001 and "Possibilities" in 2005 which is a collection of duets with numerous other performers including Annie Lennox, Sting, Paul Simon, Christina Aguilera and Carlos Santana. In 2005 Hancock toured Europe with a new quartet and also revived the Headhunters on tour.

Renowned for his many film soundtracks, Hancock is still inspired by youth culture and combines this with his efforts to balance traditional styles (using both acoustic and electric) with modern.

JAZZ *Legends*

WOODY HERMAN

Born: 16 May 1913 in Milwaukee, Wisconsin
Died: 29 October 1987 in West Hollywood, California
Instrument: Vocals/clarinet/saxophone
Suggested listening: "Woodchopper's Ball"
Trivia: Woody Herman was awarded the Grammy Lifetime Achievement Award in 1987

Woodrow "Woody" Charles Herman was born on 16 May 1913 in Milwaukee, Wisconsin. The legendary American jazz clarinettist, alto and soprano saxophonist, singer and big band leader worked as a singer in vaudeville before becoming a professional saxophone player at the age of 15. He gained his early band experience playing in Chicago alongside Tom Gerun, Harry Sosnik and on tour with Gus Arnheim. He joined Isham Jones in 1934 and when the band disbanded two years later, Herman used the leading sidemen for the formation of his own band. As a proficient swing clarinettist (and saxophonist) influenced by Johnny Hodges, Woody Herman was also a talented blues vocalist. He preferred a modern approach to music making and was never happier than when playing and creating new music.

Despite early recordings featuring Herman as a ballad vocalist, his group quickly became known as "The Band That Plays The Blues" as instrumentals became popular from the band. Mary Ann McCall provided many of the vocals but it was Billie Rogers, the female singer and trumpeter, who proved to be the main attraction for a time. Other original band members included Pete Candoli – responsible as first trumpeter for the band's screaming ensembles – Bill Harris on trombone, Flip Phillips on tenor sax, Chubby Jackson and Dave Tough. They were soon joined by Sonny Berman and Conte Candoli and the band was considered the most exciting new big band in jazz.

The final year of the 1930s saw the release of "Woodchoppers' Ball" which became an enormous hit and a huge commercial success for Herman (who played clarinet) and other band members who included Steady Nelson on trumpet, Saxie Mansfield on saxophone, Hy White on guitar and Neal Reid on trombone. "Blue Flame" was also a huge hit as was "Dupree Blues", "Blues Upstairs And Downstairs" and "Blues In The Night". The latter featured Joe Bishop on flugelhorn, Cappy Lewis on trumpet, Walt Yoder and Frankie Carlson with Tommy Linehans on piano. The band recorded for the Decca label and enjoyed real success as a popular swing band. Count Basie and Duke Ellington were huge influences and even classical composer, Stravinsky, wrote a piece for the band called "Ebony Concerto" in 1945.

Swing was really taking off at this time and Herman recorded on Columbia Records where other featured musicians included Sonny Berman, Neil Hefti, Steady Nelson, Flip Phillips, Bill Harris, Red Norvo, Ralph Burns, Davey Tough, Don Lamond and Chubby Jackson who proved himself as the band's driving force.

JAZZ*Legends*

JAZZ*Legends*

By 1943, Chubby Jackson had joined the band following a number of changes in its members and a year later they recruited Neal Hefti, Ralph Burns, Flip Phillips and Bill Harris. Known as Herman's Herd the band received international acclaim by the mid-1940s, but Herman reformed the band in 1947 and employed four saxophonists who were famously known as the "Four Brothers". Saxophonists who became part of this brotherhood included Stan Getz, Serge Chaloff, Zoot Sims, Gene Ammons, Al Cohn, who replaced Herbie Steward, while other band members included Lou Levy, Oscar Pettiford, Terry Gibbs, Shelly Manne and Herbie Steward.

It is thought that the first Herman's Herd was disbanded so that Herman could spend more time with his wife and family amidst his wife's growing problems with alcohol and pill addictions. Sadly the second Herman's Herd, despite its more mellow sound, only lasted two years but did manage to record hits such as "Early Autumn", "Four Brothers" and "The Goof And I".

Herman continued to lead bands after the second Herd break-up, ensuring his popularity and his growing reputation as a band leader. He switched labels to Capitol in 1948 and the early to mid-1950s saw the rise of the Third Herd, which was a little more accessible and conservative than the second. Then in 1959, Herman saw success with his Thundering Herd at the Monterey Jazz Festival. The history of jazz in the UK was changed forever by the formation of the Anglo-American Herd organised by Herman in 1959. Then in 1962, the Swinging Herd was created and featured Bill Chase and Phil Wilson among others. Herman changed direction in the late 1960s and introduced the soprano saxophone to his band. He was also innovative in using jazz-rock musicians during this time.

Herman returned to straightforward jazz during the 1970s and made an appearance with the Woody Herman Orchestra with Frank Sinatra for Sinatra's *Main Event* television special and recording of the same name for Reprise Records. Herman continued to perform during the 1980s but failing health saw him hand over to Frank Tiberi before his death on 29 October 1987. Woody Herman had celebrated 50 years as a band leader one year earlier.

JAZZ*Legends*

BILLIEHOLIDAY

Born: 7 April 1915 in Philadelphia, Pennsylvania
Died: 17 July 1959 in New York
Instrument: Vocals
Suggested listening: "Lover Man"
Trivia: Although Billie Holiday played a maid in her one and only Hollywood movie (1946's New Orleans), she did get to perform with her idol Louis Armstrong

orn Eleanora Fagan on 7 April 1915 in Philadelphia to teenage parents, Billie Holiday became a phenomenal star with her unique soulful voice despite not receiving any formal training. Her songs of yesteryear, it could be argued, are as well known today as they were during Holiday's heyday in the 1940s and 1950s.

With one of the greatest jazz voices in history, the passion, pain and misery that were evident in her voice due to her difficult experiences in life wowed and moved audiences worldwide. It wasn't just Holiday's singing that was to catch the headlines though, her unfortunate relationships and heroin addiction were constantly under public scrutiny, although she maintained some strong friendships with jazz legends such as Lester Young.

Influenced heavily by Bessie Smith and Louis Armstrong, Holiday grew up in Baltimore during the 1920s. Jazz was prevalent in the city and as a teenager she eked out a meagre living singing in after-hours jazz clubs to help support her mother. Holiday's father, jazz musician, Clarence Holiday was not around much to support his daughter and she reportedly got a job at a club called Monette's in New York when she was talent spotted by the producer John Hammond in 1933.

Despite not being able to read a note of music, Holiday borrowed her professional name from screen star Billie Dove and took her father's surname, joining one of the most vibrant jazz scenes in 1930s America. Holiday's introduction to Hammond led to her first record with a studio group led by Benny Goodman. Then in 1935 her career really took off when she recorded the hits "What A Little Moonlight Can Do" and "Miss Brown To You". Having landed a recording contract of her own with Columbia, she went on to record numerous titles whereupon she met Lester Young in 1937.

A year later Count Basie hired her to sing with his band and a gruelling tour followed before she joined Artie Shaw's band in 1938, making her the first black woman to work with an all white orchestra. But this didn't come without its problems and many venues were anxious for Holiday to enter by the back door on account of her colour and the racial segregation laws in place at the time. As one of the stars of the show this was humiliating for the woman who was sowing the seeds of what jazz singing really was.

"Strange Fruit" was a track that Holiday released in 1939 through Milt Gabler's Commodore – the alternative jazz label – about the lynching of a black man. It was originally a poem written by Bronx schoolteacher Abel Meeropol and was destined to become a Holiday classic which inspired the singer to concentrate more on the moving

JAZZ*Legends*

JAZZ*Legends*

ballads that helped make her a famous icon. During two major recording sessions with Commodore in 1939 and 1944 she released hits such as "Fine And Mellow" and "Embraceable You".

Her friend Lester Young coined the nickname Lady Day and Holiday was often just referred to by contemporaries as Lady. It is alleged that Holiday first picked up the name Lady at her early clubs when co-workers noticed that she would only take tips from customers straight into her hand. Pianists that worked with her admired her sheer understanding and feel for music. Often singers run away from their accompanist, or wait to be carried, but Holiday's professionalism was far superior and her unique talent for feeling the music brought her much praise from peers and made her an unrivalled jazz singer of the time.

Between 1952 and 1959, Holiday recorded more than 100 new tracks for record label Verve. This made up about a third of her recorded work and her final studio recordings were released by the label as the posthumously entitled "Last Recordings". Her final public appearance came on 25 May 1959 at the Phoenix Theatre in Greenwich Village where – according to sources at the time – she was only able to make it through two songs. A few days later Holiday was taken to hospital in New York suffering from liver and heart disease. She died on 17 July 1959 of cirrhosis of the liver.

Holiday herself suggested that the poignant edge she exuded in her music was down to how she felt. Having been subjected to a number of sexual attacks (one at the tender age of 10) and her later arrests for heroin abuse mixed with her harsh childhood where she often suffered from hunger, it is little wonder that this legendary lady of jazz was able to sing with her heart. Despite trying to clean up Holiday never fully escaped the clutches of heroin.

A statue of Holiday stands in her memory in Baltimore, Diana Ross portrayed her in 1972's *Lady Sings The Blues* and in 1994 the US Postal Service honoured Holiday with a sponsored stamp to commemorate her life's work.

LEFT
Billie Holiday singing in the early 1950s.

BELOW
Billie Holiday in portrait.

JAZZ*Legends*

57

AL JARREAU

Born: 12 March 1940 in Milwaukee, Wisconsin
Instrument: Vocals
Suggested listening: "Moonlighting"
Trivia: Al Jarreau and George Benson's "Breezin'" was nominated for the Best R&B Performance by a Duo or Group with Vocals at the 2007 Grammy Awards

Alwyn Lopez Jarreau, popularly known as Al Jarreau, was born the son of a vicar on 12 March 1940 in Milwaukee, Wisconsin. As a five-times Grammy Award winner, his versatile vocals have made him one of the top jazz singers to emerge from the US where his first singing experiences were as part of the church choir and making harmonies with his brothers. Jarreau possesses a unique style all of his own that has brought him much acclaim for his exciting and innovative musical expression.

Despite his Grammy Awards, international music awards and other accolades, music was not the only influence in Jarreau's early life. He excelled at sports and graduated from Ripon College in 1962 with a Batchelor of Science Degree in Psychology. He then received a Master's Degree in Vocational Rehabilitation from the University of Iowa which led him to San Francisco and the start of a career in rehabilitation counselling. But music remained a firm interest and while at Ripon, Jarreau sang for fun with a group called the Indigos.

At the end of the 1960s, Al Jarreau knew that singing was his future. His natural gift for music was evident and he had been performing with the George Duke trio in a small jazz club. He moved to Los Angeles and began appearing in clubs such as Dino's, the Troubador and the Bitter End West, but soon decided to take things a step further with a move to New York.

Here he received television exposure from veterans Johnny Carson, David Frost, Merv Griffin and Mike Douglas. He also played between acts with guitarist Julio Martinez at the Improv, the famous comedy venue that would launch the careers of actors and comedians such as John Belushi, Bette Midler, Jimmie Walker and Robert Klein among others.

Warner Brothers spotted Jarreau in 1975 following his stint at the Bla Bla Café in Los Angeles and promptly signed him up whereby he soon made his critically acclaimed debut album "We Got By". The album saw Jarreau's career take off internationally and his popularity and fame soared. His exceptional music on the album won him a German Grammy Award for Best New International Soloist and was quickly followed by another award on the release of his second album "Glow".

The year of 1977 marked Jarreau's first world tour and he won the US Grammy Award for Best Jazz Vocal Performance. His reputation was growing and he won critical acclaim from *Downbeat*, *Cashbox*, *Stereo Review* and *Performance* with both readers' and critics' polls. "Look To The Rainbow", Jarreau's double live album, was taken from his world tour, while

JAZZ *Legends*

his fourth album "All Fly Home" – released a year later in 1978 – won a second Grammy Award for Best Jazz Vocal Performance.

In 1980 he released "This Time" and a year later "Breakin' Away". The latter saw Jarreau's popularity widen and he received two more Grammy Awards for Best Male Pop Vocalist and Best Male Jazz Vocal Performance. "Breakin' Away" was one of his most artistically and commercially successful albums and included the hit "We're In This Love Together". 1983 brought two new albums, "Jarreau" and "High Crime", which provided numerous R&B and pop hits. This brought him further recognition worldwide and his follow up, "Al Jarreau Live In London" (recorded at Wembley Arena in 1985) cemented his international reputation and his place in the history books.

With his ability to master both stage and studio and his uncanny imitations of guitar, bass and percussion, Jarreau had certainly proved himself on the world stage by the mid-1980s.

He then collaborated with top producer Nile Rodgers on "L Is For Lover" where he tried new styles and sounds. His popularity and career went from strength to strength and Jarreau wrote and performed the theme to *Moonlighting* starring Cybil Shepherd and Bruce Willis which was Grammy nominated. He earned another Grammy nomination for his album "Heart's Horizon" which included the Number 2 hit "So Good".

For two years Jarreau toured the world before heading back to the US and a recording studio. He released "Heaven And Earth", produced by Narada Michael Walden, in 1992 which won him his fifth Grammy with an award for Best R&B Vocal Performance. This Grammy Award was to see him become one of the rare artists that have received Grammys for different musical genres – in Jarreau's case – jazz, R&B and pop.

Jarreau released "Tenderness" in 1994 where he stars with the likes of David Sanborn and Kathleen Battle to name but a few, producing classics and contemporary tracks alike. Two years later and Jarreau was trying something new in the form of a stint on Broadway as the Teen Angel in the musical *Grease*. "The Best Of Al Jarreau" was released to celebrate 20 years of success which also includes two new tracks by George Duke. "Tomorrow Today" was released in 2000 and includes a duet with Vanessa Williams in "God's Gift To The World".

As one of the most prolific singers of his generation, Al Jarreau has been rewarded with a star on the Hollywood Walk of Fame.

JOHN
McLAUGHLIN

Born: 4 January 1942 in Doncaster, Yorkshire
Instrument: Guitar
Suggested listening: "My Goals Beyond"
Trivia: John McLaughlin was a notable follower of guru Sri Chinmoy, as was Carlos Santana

Legendary jazz guitarist, John McLaughlin – born on 4 January 1942 in Doncaster, Yorkshire – made his name with Miles Davis's electric jazz fusion groups in the late 1960s producing such greats as "A Tribute To Jack Johnson". He first joined Georgie Fame's band, the Blue Flames before joining the Graham Bond Organisation and then Brian Auger's Trinity. He formed his own band in 1968.

In 1969 he recorded "Extrapolation" in collaboration with John Surman and Tony Oxley where his talents in terms of sheer virtuosity became evident to all. Later that same year, he moved to the US to join Lifetime, Tony Williams's group, a band that had a great impact on the US jazz scene. The US was where he met Davis and he became involved in the albums "In A Silent Way", "Bitches Brew" and "Big Fun". Davis was particularly impressed with McLaughlin's solos and "Bitches Brew" features a song with his name. McLaughlin became a regular sideman for Wayne Shorter, the Rolling Stones, Miroslav Vitous, Larry Coryell and Carla Bley among others. He also returned to Davis's band for two recorded gigs which took place during a week-long club contract and resulted in the album "Live/Evil".

McLaughlin teamed up with violinist Jerry Goodman and drummer Billy Cobham in order to make an album which showed the acoustic guitar to its best advantage. "My Goals Beyond" was recorded by the trio and was critically acclaimed.

Renowned for being probably one of the greatest guitarists in the world, McLaughlin also earned a reputation with his acclaimed Mahavishnu Orchestra which although quite short lived was an intense musical experience for the artist during the early 1970s. The group were famous for their blend of Eastern and Indian influences fused with eclectic jazz and rock which were played with a complex style and technical virtuosity. Band members included Goodman, Cobham, Rick Laird and Jan Hammer. Future band members would include Jean-Luc Ponty, Gayle Moran, Stu Goldberg, Ralphe Armstrong and Narada Michael Walden. The band firmly established fusion as a new and upcoming style which would go on to greatly influence jazz and rock music worldwide.

McLaughlin's vision was to be able to play music and provide inspiration in the same way that John Coltrane achieved on the saxophone. Few critics would deny that he has achieved this and his is comparable to the likes of Wes Montgomery and Charlie Christian who went before him. McLaughlin was undoubtedly inspired by these and other great

JAZZ*Legends*

guitarists, but he was looking to elevate jazz guitar to new heights in the way that progressive jazz musicians such as Coltrane and Omette Coleman achieved. The result when he reached this point was sensational.

McLaughlin quickly established himself as one of the most versatile and influential guitarists of all time and was also a master composer of classical jazz fusion pieces. McLaughlin then established the group Shakti which was his way of furthering his groundbreaking innovations. The idea was to produce elements of jazz that were fused with Indian music leading to McLaughlin becoming the first westerner to attain critical acclaim with Indian audiences.

The band won further acclaim worldwide for their mix of East and West musical traditions. He then worked with artists such as Chick Corea and David Sanborn on "Johnny McLaughlin Electric Guitarist" and Katia Labeque on "Music Spoken here" before joining up with peers Paco de Lucia and Al Di Meola on "Passion Grace And Fire" and "Friday Night In San Francisco".

Ernest Fleishman, director of the Los Angeles Philharmonic, commissioned McLaughlin to write "Mediterranean", a guitar concerto which was first performed in 1985. McLaughlin as a soloist received rave reviews from critics and the first night's performance earned him a standing ovation. Conducted by the legendary Michael Tilson Thomas and played by the London Symphony Orchestra (LSO), the concerto was released by CBS Masterworks in early 1990. A second concerto was commissioned by the Deutsche Kammerphilharmonic and performed during a tour of Europe.

McLaughlin teamed up with Trilok Gurtu, the percussionist, and Dominique Di Piazza in 1988 and formed the John McLaughlin Trio, touring worldwide for five consecutive years and recording "Live At The Royal Festival Hall" and "Que Allegria" in 1990 and 1992 respectively. He toured with new band the Free Spirits in 1993 and recorded "Time Remembered, John McLaughlin Plays Bill Evans" with six acoustic guitars in honour of the man who much inspired him – Bill Evans. "After The Rain" in 1995 was dedicated to another hero of McLaughlin, John Coltrane.

McLaughlin released "Thieves And Poets" in 2003 which is a ballet score, various classical guitar recordings and a DVD instructional pack on improvisation. "Industrial Zen" is a hard bop/jazz fusion album which sees the composer and virtuoso experimenting with the Godin Glissentar.

JAZZ*Legends*

GLENN
MILLER

Born: 1 March 1904 in Clarinda, Iowa
Died: 15 December 1944 over the English Channel
Instrument: Trombone
Suggested listening: "Moonlight Serenade"
Trivia: A Norseman plane was discovered off the coast of northern France in 1985 but was unidentifiable and did not contain any human remains

G lenn Miller was undeniably a man of the people in that his music was approachable and enjoyed by the masses. This did not particularly bring him critical acclaim, but his influence on jazz during the 1940s ensured his place in history, while his music is still enjoyed by listeners today.

Born as Alton Glenn Miller in Clarinda, Iowa, on 1 March 1904, Miller's "Moonlight Serenade", written while he was still studying music with Dr Schillinger in New York became famous worldwide. As a trombonist and band leader, Miller defied his critics and became a jazz legend dedicating his life to producing music that was designed to entertain.

Three years after his birth, Miller's parents moved to Nebraska where evenings were filled with his mother, Mattie Lou, playing a simple pump organ. She started a school called Happy Hollow before the family moved in 1915 to Grant City, Missouri. It was here that Miller took up the trombone and played for bandsman John Mosbarger. Miller discovered an interest and a talent for football while at high school in Fort Morgan, Colorado, but his increasing fascination with dance band music led him and some friends to start their own band.

In 1921 Miller joined the Boyd Senter Band but left two years later to attend the University of Colorado. After university he joined Ben Pollack's band before moving to New York City in 1928 to work as a trombonist and arranger. He married Helen Burger and started working for the Dorsey Brothers Orchestra. He then organised the Ray Noble Orchestra while studying composition and theory with Joseph Schillinger.

He first recorded under his own name in 1934 and then in 1937 he formed his own band which turned out to be unsuccessful. But a year later, after forming a new band, Miller found success with a gig at the Glen Island Casino, in New Rochelle, New York. Singers in the band included Ray Eberle, Marion Hutton, Paula Kelly, Dorothy Claire and the Modernaires, while band members consisted of Tex Beneke, Chummy MacGregor, Billy May, Clyde Hurley, Al Klink, Johnny Best, Ernie Caceres, Ray Anthony, Maurice Purtill, Wilbur Schwartz, Hal McIntyre and Bobby Hackett among many others.

Commercial success and popularity rose in the following years up to 1942 with the Glenn Miller Orchestra having 17 Top 10 hits in the US in 1939, 31 in 1940 and 11 hits in 1941 and 1942. As well as "Moonlight Serenade", other popular tracks included "A String Of Pearls", "In The Mood" and "Little Brown Jug". Entitled *Moonlight Serenade*, Miller

found further acclaim with his popular radio series which was aired on CBS three times a week. It was around this time that another avenue opened up for Miller – the movies. His band worked on *Sun Valley Serenade* producing the hit "Chattanooga Choo Choo" in 1941 and "Kalamazoo" for *Orchestra Wives* a year later.

The secret of Miller's success has to be the unique sound and style of his band. Favouring orchestration as opposed to improvisation, Miller's band was synonymous with swing and brought structure and meticulous preparation to their music which was less than popular with his critics. However, his audiences loved it and the band was set apart from others of the time. Clarinet and saxophone were combined to give a resonant sound in the melodies where other saxophones were used to provide the harmony. This was a far cry from the likes of contemporary bands who favoured the sax belting out solos with virtuoso improvisations.

Miller put his musical career on hold to serve his country during World War II. Too old, aged 38, to be drafted into the Navy he enlisted in the US Army Air Force in 1942 to become Captain in the Army Specialist Corp where he maintained his musical talents by modernising the band. Miller and his band of 50 members became instrumental in keeping up troops' morale with a hectic schedule of tours giving over 800 performances. Miller also hosted the weekly radio show *Sustain The Wings*. Fatefully, on 15 December 1944, Miller boarded a C-64 single engine Norseman bound for Paris. Miller had been due to make arrangements for a Christmas broadcast. The plane set off over the English Channel but tragically never arrived at its destination and was never found. Miller was just 40 years old.

The band played the Christmas concert under the direction of Jerry Gray and played their last concert on 13 November 1945 at the National Press Club dinner for President Truman in Washington DC. Miller's willingness to give up his lucrative band and serve with the US Army Air Force, bringing joy to service men and women, has earned this legendary jazz musician a place in history as a true musical patriot.

LEFT
Glenn Miller conducting a concert during WWII.

BELOW
Glenn Miller pictured with his trombone.

JAZZ*Legends*

CHARLIE**MINGUS**

Born: 22 April 1922 in Nogales, Arizona
Died: 5 January 1979 in Cuernavaca, Mexico
Instrument: Double bass/piano
Suggested listening: "Epitaph"
Trivia: After his death, Charlie Mingus's ashes were scattered in the River Ganges

orn on 22 April 1922, Charles Mingus, despite being prone to depression, was an all time great jazz bassist, composer and band leader of the 20th century. Although born in Nogales, Arizona, Mingus was raised in Los Angeles and was exposed to church music at home – which is all his mother would allow.

He learnt the trombone and later the cello, but his passion for jazz, particularly Duke Ellington's music, led him to take up the double bass in high school. His advanced compositions during his teen years were later recorded in 1960 and were released in the album "Pre-bird" (a reference to Charlie "Bird" Parker). He became something of a bass prodigy and began touring with Louis Armstrong in 1943 before joining Lionel Hampton's band in the late 1940s. But it was his trio with Red Norvo and Tal Farlow from 1950-51 that brought the young musician critical acclaim.

He briefly joined Ellington's band in the early 1950s but was reportedly fired by Ellington himself for his temper – something he became notorious for. He was nicknamed "The angry man of jazz" by his peers and was prone to onstage outbursts. Despite being fired by the great man himself, Mingus's admiration for Duke Ellington never waned and he continued to be influenced by this innovator.

Mingus gained the opportunity to play a number of gigs with another great jazz inspiration, Charlie Parker. Mingus was greatly influenced by Parker's compositions and he considered him the greatest innovator in jazz. But Mingus was confused by his relationship with Parker and despised the musician's self-destructive habits and drug addiction which often involved luring in other jazz musicians to self-destruct. Mingus famously wrote the song "If Charlie Parker Were A Gunslinger, There'd Be A Whole Lot Of Dead Copycats".

The year of 1952 saw Mingus co-found Debut Records with Max Roach. The idea behind this was so Mingus could record in his own way. He joined Dizzy Gillespie, Charlie Parker, Roach and Bud Powell at the 1953 live recording of a concert at Massey Hall after Oscar Pettiford broke his arm.

The recordings are regarded as some of the best live jazz recordings ever made, despite being Debut Records' earliest releases. Mingus later over-dubbed his bass part (which in his view was not prominent enough). A gig in 1955 featuring Mingus, Roach, Parker and Powell became infamous when Bud Powell was helped from the stage unable to play or speak coherently having suffered from alcohol abuse and mental illness over many years.

JAZZ*Legends*

Parker took a microphone and began to chant Powell's name for several minutes. Incensed by the whole incident, Mingus took another microphone and asked the audience to disassociate him with what was taking place.

Mingus enjoyed his breakthrough year in 1956 with the release of his album "Pithecanthropus Erectus" which was regarded as his first major album both as a composer and band leader. Up to this point he had recorded a number of albums as band leader, but this new album was written with certain musicians in mind including Jackie McLean on sax and Mal Waldron on piano. It was a mix of blues and complicated compositions including its title track which is a 10-minute tone poem.

Mingus's compositions were often unconventional. He was heavily influenced by gospel music and hard bop, but also brought free jazz and Third Stream Jazz (fusing classical music with mainstream jazz) into his compositions. He was also inspired by the New Orleans jazz of the early 1920s along with groundbreaking improvisation and chose to create a unique style of music which he intended to be played by outstanding musicians who understood his music.

Mingus was also renowned for writing for individual musicians' abilities, highlighting strengths and creating a seamless interaction throughout his band. He favoured a mid-sized ensemble of around eight to 10 players and created the "Jazz Workshop", a group of jazz musicians he particularly admired, often little known players, who were seeking the limelight.

But the workshop was not an easy ride for these wannabes and Mingus constantly pushed his musicians to develop and explore. Such was Mingus's influence that the workshop became known as the "University for Jazz". Many of these young musicians, including Horace Parlan, Jimmy Knepper, Pepper Adams and Jaki Byard went on to have high profile careers.

Dannie Richmond who featured on Mingus's album "The Clown" in 1957 was to remain with his band until the band leader's death more than 20 years later. Drummer and bassist formed one of the most impressive rhythm sections of the 20th century. When later joined by Jaki Byard on piano the trio became known as "The Almighty Three".

At the time of his death on 5 January 1979, Mingus had been recording with singer Joni Mitchell. He was an activist against racial injustice all his life.

JAZZ*Legends*

THELONIOUS
MONK

Born: 10 October 1917 in Rocky Mount, North Carolina
Died: 17 February 1982 in New York
Instrument: Piano
Suggested listening: "'Round Midnight"
Trivia: North Coast Brewery brews a beer named Brother Thelonious in honour of Thelonious Monk.

Thelonious Sphere Monk was set to influence the history of jazz. Born on 10 October 1917, in Rocky Mount, North Carolina, Monk went on to become recognised as one of the leading greats whose music both as a composer and pianist would inspire and influence almost every genre of music.

Monk's family moved to New York while he was still young and he took up piano lessons with his sister's teacher but, despite this, remained mainly self-taught. By the age of 13 he had won a weekly amateur contest at the Apollo Theatre so frequently that he was banned from entering the competition. His improvised style was so unique that his successors have been unable to come close to imitating his style.

Some of his best known works include the albums "Round Midnight" and "Blue Monk". Credited with being one of the architects of bebop, along with Dizzy Gillespie and Charlie Parker, to name just two, Monk rarely displayed this style in his own music, preferring dissonant harmony and the dramatic use of silences during his improvisations.

Giving up his place at the Peter Stuyvesant High School he began touring with a local evangelist during his teenage years playing the church organ, but he left to begin his career in jazz and became one of the most inventive pianists ever by creating a musical vision that was quite simply ahead of its time. He was a musical prodigy who formed his own quartet in 1937 touring local bars and clubs.

Then in 1941, he was hired as the house pianist at Minton's Playhouse in Harlem by drummer Kenny Clarke. As part of the after-hours jam sessions it is likely that Monk was indeed a part of the bebop revolution taking place. But, Monk was already taking a different path with his music with his unusual repetition of phrases, dissonant harmonies and offbeat use of pauses and silences. Utilising the entire keyboard with both hands – which was not typical of the sparse left-hand chords of the bebop style – Monk's music did not adhere to the fast and ferocious virtuosic solos of the time and he was more inclined to be economical with his notes. His composition style was more about creating a whole new architecture for music where melody, chords and rhythm moulded together. He was to revolutionise modern music with his progressive style and unique sound.

Monk made his first recordings for Blue Note in 1947 and that same year married his sweetheart, Nellie Smith. He spent most of the early to mid-1950s composing and recording as well as playing out of town gigs and theatres due to the loss of his Cabaret

JAZZ *Legends*

JAZZ *Legends*

Card. The police confiscated the card when Monk refused to testify against his friend and co-musician Bud Powell who had been found with drugs in his car.

After intermittent recordings for Blue Note, Monk signed with Prestige Records in 1952 where he made some little-known albums with Sonny Rollins and Art Blakey. Then in 1954 he took part in the famed Christmas Eve sessions before embarking on his first visit to Europe where he performed and recorded in Paris. His innovative music was deemed difficult and many of his records did not sell in high numbers so Riverside Records were able to buy out Monk's contract from Prestige for a small fee. It was Riverside who managed to persuade Monk to compromise and to record two albums with his own interpretations on classic jazz standards. This was to prove his breakthrough. The album "Thelonious Monk Plays Duke Ellington" was cleverly designed to make him more accessible to a wider audience, and so pave the way for his unique style to become more acceptable.

In June 1957 with his Cabaret Card restored, Monk re-launched his New York career with a six-month gig at the Five Spot Café, leading a quartet including John Coltrane. Although the group did perform at Carnegie Hall, there is little else known about Monk's band.

LEFT
Thelonious Monk
in portrait.

BELOW
A coat worn by
Thelonious Monk on
display, 2005.

By 1964, Monk was signed to Columbia Records which brought him greater recognition. He still had a regular working group but his compositional work had largely dried up and only his final album "Underground" featured a large number of new tracks including "Ugly Beauty". By the early 1970s he had almost all but disappeared from the scene and only made a small number of appearances throughout the remainder of his life.

His final tour took place in 1971 where it was reported that he had almost given up speaking to anyone other than his beloved wife Nellie. It was reported that he had suffered from mental illness towards the end of his life although no diagnosis was ever made public. He died of a stroke on 17 February 1982. He was posthumously awarded a Pulitzer Prize for Music "Special Citation" in 2006.

JAZZ*Legends*

CHARLIE**PARKER**

Born: 29 August 1920 in Kansas City, Kansas
Died: 12 March 1955 in New York
Instrument: Saxophone
Suggested listening: "Billie's Bounce"
Trivia: Charlie Parker abused his body so much that the coroner estimated him as being between 50 and 60 years old at the time of his death

Charles "Bird" Parker, more popularly known as Charlie, was born on 29 August 1920 and went on to become one of the most influential musicians on the American jazz scene during a prolific and exciting period for the musical genre. Famous for his improvisations on the saxophone and a pivotal figure in the development of bebop (due to late night jamming sessions at Minton's Playhouse and Monroe's Uptown House in New York), Parker inspired a generation of jazz performers and composers.

When he was seven years old, Parker's family moved to Kansas City, Missouri where African-American music was prevalent and important throughout the 1920s and 1930s. He took up the alto saxophone in 1933 and managed to land gigs with semi-professional groups – there is no evidence to suggest that Parker showed any particular musical promise as a child – before he left school in 1935. For the next four years, he worked in and around Kansas City with a variety of local jazz and blues groups and, like most of his contemporaries, Parker learned his skill through practical experience.

In 1939, New York City was the capital of jazz and this is where Parker headed for the next 12 months working sporadically as a musician. Jam sessions were readily available to him however and he took up the opportunity to participate regularly. He then played for Jay McShann's band from 1940-42 which saw him tour Chicago, New York and the Southwest US. This period also marked the start of his recording career (in 1941) which showcased Parker's unique swing style.

Despite his lack of experience and somewhat conventional style his improvisation potential was evident in these first recordings which were made for broadcasts of the time. He was hired by Earl Hines's big band in December 1942 and he became a co-band member along with Dizzy Gillespie. In May, two years later, the beginnings of Billy Eckstine's band had been formed.

Parker was able to "hear" what he wanted to do with his instrument, but found himself unable to technically achieve it when playing. However, a session with guitarist Biddy Fleet changed that when Parker discovered that by using the higher intervals of a chord for the melody and using appropriate changes he could achieve the style and vision that he was looking for. But his own unique style did not really emerge until around 1944-45 when his rhythm and phrasing had considerably matured.

His regular jamming sessions at both Minton's Playhouse and Monroe's Uptown House in New York City offered Parker the chance to develop and expand his style in an informal

atmosphere. Bebop was happening and the small groups that met for these jamming sessions were instrumental in developing the new style. A strike by the American Federation of Musicians virtually all but silenced the recording industry between August 1942-44 and Parker re-emerged first as a sideman in 1944 and a year later as a band leader which afforded him the opportunity to present his music to a wider audience for the first time. 1945 also marked a turning point.

Parker and Gillespie began working with small groups and in December 1945 the two jazz legends headed for Hollywood where they fulfilled a six-week gig at a nightclub. Parker kept working until June 1946 when a nervous breakdown forced him to be admitted to hospital where he was treated for his addiction to heroin and alcohol. He was back working in January 1947 when he formed a quintet with Miles Davis, Tommy Potter, Duke Jordan and Max Roach recording many of his most famous pieces and he visited Europe at the end of the 1940s.

Up until 1951 Parker enjoyed his most prolific period but his ongoing problems with drugs and alcohol brought about the confiscation of his Cabaret Card at the request of the narcotics squad. Unable to play at gigs where alcohol was served, Parker was forced into a low key life until 1953 when he was given back his card. Despite having enjoyed some commercial success, Parker was by now badly in debt and failing in health both physically and mentally. He twice attempted suicide and voluntarily committed himself to the Bellevue Hospital in New York in 1954.

Some of his most famous songs include "Billie's Bounce" and "Anthropology" while those influenced by this great man include John Coltrane and the cello virtuoso Yo-Yo Ma. His wife – Chan Parker – wrote an autobiography about her family and her life with "Bird", *My Life In E Flat*, which is an intimate and touchingly human account of life with the jazz icon.

On 5 March 1955 he appeared in his last public performance at Birdland – a nightclub in New York named in his honour – with Bud Powell and Charlie Mingus. Seven days later he died aged 34 of pneumonia aided by drug and alcohol complications.

JAZZ *Legends*

BUDDY**RICH**

Born: 30 September 1917 in Brooklyn, New York
Died: 2 April 1987 in Los Angeles, California
Instrument: Drums/percussion
Suggested listening: "I'll Never Be The Same"
Trivia: Buddy Rich appeared on the Parkinson chat show just a few weeks prior to his death

C hild prodigy, Bernard "Buddy" Rich became one of the world's most outstanding drummers of all time. Influenced by the likes of Louie Bellson and the playing of Gene Krupa, Joe Jones and Chick Webb, Rich quickly established himself on the drums when he was propelled into the limelight during the swing era while playing for the likes of the Artie Shaw and Tommy Dorsey big bands. His most prolific era came during the 1950s although the 1960s saw him front a popular big band until his death in 1987, despite competition from the rock and pop genres.

Born on 30 September 1917 in Brooklyn, New York, Rich's talents were first spotted by his father when, aged one, he demonstrated his rhythmical talents with two spoons. He was billed as "Traps The Drum Wonder" aged 18 months when he appeared playing drums in vaudeville. He was also a regular at the age of four on Broadway. It was reported later in his childhood that he was the highest paid child star after Jackie Coogan (the silent movie actor). Rich led his first band aged 11, despite having no formal drum training, and claimed never to practice. He advocated that he only played during performances.

Rich first joined Joe Marsala's band in 1937 before linking up with Bunny Berigan in 1938 and Artie Shaw a year later. Even though he'd had no instruction himself, in 1939, Rich began teaching a young Mel Brooks how to play the drums and persuaded Shaw to allow the 13-year-old to attend recording sessions in Manhattan. He was connected to Tommy Dorsey for three periods, 1939-42, 1945 and 1954-55 while also playing for Benny Carter, Harry James, Les Brown and Charlie Ventura as well as Jazz at the Philharmonic concerts. Rich was busy as a band leader and also performed in other prestigious groups at this time. He played with Dizzy Gillespie, Louis Armstrong and Gene Krupa and appeared in the films *Symphony Of Swing* in 1939, *Ship Ahoy* and *How's About It* in 1942 and 1943 respectively.

Rich had a successful career that was set to span seven decades, where his dexterity and incredible speed, combined with a natural sense of rhythm made him an undisputed star. Throughout the 1960s and 1970s, Rich toured with his own bands and had incredible success with the big band set-up despite the demise of this style of music for other jazz musicians as the popularity of rock and pop took hold. He also opened two nightclubs, Buddy's Place and Buddy's Place II which allowed him to play for his fans. Both venues were usually full with audiences clamouring to hear the virtuosic drummer. Buddy's Place

JAZZ*Legends*

II became the venue that Rich used to experiment with new styles and where he began introducing more elements of rock into his repertoire. This change in direction brought him critical acclaim as a great rock drummer.

Rich became a regular on television talk shows including those of Johnny Carson, Mike Douglas, Dick Cavett and Merv Griffin. Known for his caustic wit, he was ever popular with television and studio audiences alike. Unlike many musicians of his generation who received a stinging review from Downbeat, Rich actually won an award as well as many, many other awards and accolades too numerous to mention. Rich was also an international icon and became popular for his *West Side Story* medley and big band arrangement for Leonard Bernstein's classic musical, as well as for his worldwide tours which often included playing for world leaders and, of course, presidents of his home country including, Roosevelt, J F Kennedy and Reagan.

Rich was renowned for being a mild-natured musician, but he was also prone to having a short temper at times. He would hold his power over musicians in his band by threatening to fire them, but this very rarely happened and he was keen during interviews to praise the musicians who worked with him. Some band members secretly recorded some of his outbursts which were sold on.

On a lighter note, Rich famously appeared on *The Muppets* where he performed an outstanding duet with "Animal" on the drums. Before this, Rich is seen walking around the Muppet set playing with his drum sticks on the banisters, the lights and the walls where he quotes: "When I play the theatre, I really play the theatre".

Rich died on 2 April 1987 of heart failure after surgery to remove a brain tumour. During his stay in hospital, the only thing that Rich said he was allergic to was country music. Despite their many fallings-out on stage, long-time friend, Frank Sinatra gave an extremely moving eulogy at Rich's funeral.

In 1994, a tribute album "Burning For Buddy: A Tribute To The Music Of Buddy Rich" was released and there have been several memorial concerts held in his name. A second tribute album was released in 1997.

NINA
SIMONE

Born: 21 February 1933 in Tryone, North Carolina
Died: 21 April 2003 in Carry-le-Rouet, France
Instrument: Vocals/piano
Suggested listening: "My Baby Just Cares For Me"
Trivia: Nina Simone's version of "House Of The Rising Sun" proved to be both an inspiration and a signature tune for 1960s group the Animals

Having studied at the prestigious Julliard School of Music in New York, Nina Simone became one of the most outstanding jazz singers of her generation and reputedly of the 20th century. Her vocal qualities are still enjoyed by listeners today and appear timeless. Artists still make cover versions of her songs and much of her music has been featured in soundtracks for motion pictures. Advertising companies use her music in commercials while other work is frequently heard in remixes.

Born Eunice Kathleen Waymon on 21 February 1933, in Tryone, North Carolina, Nina Simone – as she became popularly known – was the sixth of eight children born into a poor family. She showed early promise on the piano at the age of four and with the help of her teacher set up the Eunice Waymon Fund so that she could be educated. Simone began singing at her local church and made her public debut aged 10 when she gave a piano recital. Her own parents, who had sat in the front row, were made to move to the back so that they could make way for white members of the audience. Simone refused to start the recital until her parents were moved back. It was probably this incident that championed her move to become involved in civil rights.

Aged 17, Simone moved to Philadelphia where she taught piano and accompanied singers to fund her studies at the Julliard as well as to provide some financial support for her family. She was rejected by the Curtis Institute and Simone strongly believed this was because she was black. Denied a place at the Institute, Simone – who was set to become the first African-American classical pianist – found that her career path changed direction.

She found herself working at a bar in Atlantic City where the owner said she would have to sing as well. She adopted the stage name Nina Simone and embarked on a career that combined jazz and blues as well as classical music. She went on to play in other local bars before recording a rendition of Gershwin's "I Loves You Porgy" in 1958. This led to her first album "Little Girl Blue" with Bethlehem Records – which includes the hit single "My Baby Just Cares For Me" (a UK Top 5 hit when re-released in the 1980s) – and a gig at Carnegie Hall as well as the Newport Jazz Festival. Despite her music containing a mix of gospel and spiritual songs as well as folk songs and pop, Simone became synonymous with jazz, although this branding was not particularly favoured by the great lady herself.

With her ability to combine the counterpoint of Bach, the improvisation of jazz and the soulful blues, Simone's talent was breathtaking. Her audiences were spellbound where her versatility as a singer, pianist, dancer and actress were evident to all. She also enjoyed the

JAZZ*Legends*

monologues and dialogues that she treated her audiences to and, like Thelonious Monk before her, was inclined to use pauses and spaces in her music.

Simone became deeply aware of the severity of racial prejudice in the US. Her move from recording label American Colpix to Dutch Philips enabled her to produce an album "Nina Simone In Concert" in 1964 which openly addressed the racial inequality being experienced across the States with the track "Mississippi Goddam". Simone recorded this bitter song as a reaction to the killing of four black children in a church bombing in Birmingham, Alabama in 1963.

From this point on, many of Simone's most famous hits were aimed at racial intolerance and the civil rights issues that she so vehemently supported. Also known affectionately as the High Priestess of Soul, Simone was often greatly misunderstood. Her song "Four Women" in 1966 was a bitter lament of four black women whose circumstances and outlook are related to subtle gradations in skin colour, however, several radio networks denied the song air time because it was thought that the song was insulting to black people. She registered her highest UK chart entry in 1968 with the Number 2 "Ain't Got No – I Got Life"/"Do What You Gotta Do" and her 1969 album "Nina Simone And Piano" came as a surprise to most when there was no band. But the album, a collection of songs about reincarnation, death, loneliness and love is undoubtedly a highlight in her career.

In 1970 Simone left the US for Barbados where miscommunication with her husband and manager, Andrew Stroud, meant that their marriage ended in divorce. With no idea what she was worth and no real knowledge of how her affairs were run, Simone discovered that she had problems with the US tax authorities. After temporary stays in various other countries, Simone eventually settled in France in 1992 – the same year that her autobiography *I Put a Spell on You* was published – and produced her last album "A Single Woman" in 1993.

Simone died of cancer on 21 April 1993 aged 70 and the world lost a great legend of jazz.

LEFT
Nina Simone in concert, 1991.

BELOW
Nina Simone in portrait.

JAZZ *Legends*

FATS**WALLER**

Born: 21 May 1904 in Passaic, New Jersey
Died: 15 December 1943 near Kansas City, Missouri
Instrument: Piano
Suggested listening: "Ain't Misbehavin'"
Trivia: Though Waller could read and write music, his improvisations have had to be transcribed from old recordings and radio broadcasts

Fats (so nicknamed because of his 300lb weight) Waller – born Thomas Wright Waller on 21 May 1904 in Passaic, New Jersey – was the son of a Baptist minister who learned to play the organ in church with his mother. His father held open-air services in Harlem and the youngster soon became accustomed to performing in front of an audience, playing a reed organ. Fats's grandfather, Adolph Waller, was an accomplished violinist so it was no surprise when his grandson displayed a similar musical talent.

He won a talent contest in 1918 playing James P Johnson's "Carolina Shout", a song he had learned by watching a pianola play, and by the following year was installed as the organist of the Lincoln Theatre on 135th Street. Opposing his father's wish for him to carve out a religious career, Waller moved in with fellow pianist Russell BT Brooks after his mother's death in 1920 and later took piano lessons from Johnson.

Fats began his recording career in 1922 with "Muscle Shoals Blues" and made a living making piano rolls (including "Got To Cool My Doggies Now"), playing rent parties, as an organist at movie theatres and accompanying various vaudeville acts. He collaborated with the likes of Sara Martin, Alberta Hunter and Maude Mills and the following year Clarence Williams recorded Waller's "Wild Cat Blues" with his Blue Five. Gaining a reputation as a composer, Waller began making radio appearances but continued his stint at the Lincoln Theatre, adding the Lafayette Theatre to his resumé.

He perfected and expanded the style known as Stride, descended from ragtime, but incorporating a more elaborate and decorative approach. Indeed, Waller is acknowledged to be one of the three masters of this style of play, along with his tutor Johnson and Willie "the Lion" Smith who gave Fats the nickname Filthy.

Fats Waller was such an impressive and talented pianist that he came to the attention of the rich, famous…and notorious! In 1926 after a performance in Chicago, Waller was allegedly kidnapped by four men, bundled into a car and driven to the Hawthorne Inn. Pushed into the establishment at gunpoint and ordered to start playing the piano, a frightened Waller then realised he had been "booked" to perform at the owner's birthday party…Al Capone. He eventually left, so the story goes, very tired and very drunk three days later.

In 1927 Waller co-wrote some tunes with James P Johnson for his show *Keep Shufflin'* and, two years later, wrote the score for the Broadway hit *Hot Chocolates* with lyrics supplied by Tin Pan Alley lyricist and friend Andy Razaf. This show introduced Waller's

best known song, "Ain't Misbehavin'", to the waiting world delivered first by Cab Calloway and then Louis Armstrong.

Waller's big opportunity came after being signed to Victor Records and he recorded "St Louis Blues" and "Lenox Avenue Blues". He recorded with numerous artists including Morris's Hot Babes, Fats Waller's Buddies (one of the earliest interracial groups to record) and McKinney's Cotton Pickers. In 1929, Waller immortalised the Stride piano style with the self-penned "Handful Of Keys", "Smashing Thirds", "Numb Fumblin'" and "Valentine Stomp".

His greatest success, however, came with his own five- or six-piece band named Fats Waller and his Rhythm, consisting of half a dozen musicians who worked with him regularly, including Herman Autrey, Bill Coleman, John "Bugs" Hamilton, Gene Sedric, Rudy Powell and Al Casey.

In the mid-1930s, Waller worked with Les Hite's band at Frank Sebastian's New Cotton Club on the West Coast, finding the time to appear in two films; *Hooray For Love!* and *King Of Burlesque*. His first European tour in 1938 proved to be a success, but a return the following year was dramatically cut short by the outbreak of World War II.

The early 1940s proved to be a very busy time for Waller, with recording sessions, domestic tours, radio shows and composing taking up much of his time. He also made another film, *Stormy Weather*, with Lena Horne and Bill Robinson in early 1943. This extreme workload, coupled with his overeating and excessive drinking, undoubtedly contributed to his death on 15 December 1943. Having been taken ill while completing an engagement at Hollywood's Zanzibar Room, Waller died of pneumonia on the train journey home.

Not that that was the end of the Fats Waller story, as his music will never be forgotten. As well as those mentioned previously, he is responsible for giving the world such classics as "Squeeze Me", "Keepin' Out Of Mischief Now", "Blue Turning Grey Over You", "Honeysuckle Rose", "I've Got A Feeling I'm Falling" and "Jitterbug Waltz". A Broadway musical entitled *Ain't Misbehavin'* showcasing Waller's songs opened in the Longacre Theatre in 1978 and included such songs as "Honeysuckle Rose", "The Joint Is Jumpin'", and "Ain't Misbehavin'".

LEFT
Fats Waller in his favourite place, at the piano.

BELOW
Fats Waller was brilliant at improvising.

JAZZ *Legends*

ALSO AVAILABLE IN THIS SERIES

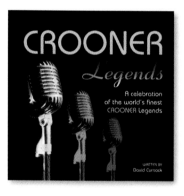

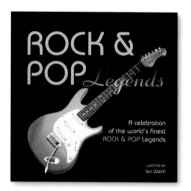

THE PICTURES IN THIS BOOK WERE PROVIDED COURTESY OF THE FOLLOWING:

GETTYIMAGES
101 Bayham Street, London NW1 0AG

Concept and Creative Direction:
VANESSA and KEVINGARDNER

Design and Artwork: KEVINGARDNER

Image research: ELLIECHARLESTON

PUBLISHED BY GREEN UMBRELLA PUBLISHING

Publishers:
JULESGAMMOND and VANESSAGARDNER

Written by: CLAIREWELCH